KNOCK-KNOCK ROCKS!

MORE THAN [illegible] KIDS!

SUPER-FUNNY

ROFL

JOKES

Tommy NELSON®

An Imprint of Thomas Nelson

Super-Funny ROFL Jokes

© 2019 by Thomas Nelson

Published in Nashville, Tennessee, by Tommy Nelson. Tommy Nelson is an imprint of Thomas Nelson. Thomas Nelson is a registered trademark of HarperCollins Christian Publishing, Inc.

Tommy Nelson titles may be purchased in bulk for educational, business, fund-raising, or sales promotional use. For information, please e-mail SpecialMarkets@ThomasNelson.com.

Jokes by Tommy Marshall.

Printed in the United States of America

19 20 21 22 23   LSC   10 9 8 7 6 5 4 3 2 1

Mfr: LSC / Crawfordsville, Indiana / October 2019 / PO # 9553793

Contents

Jokes, Jokes, and More Jokes

Q: What's the only kind of shoes frogs will wear?

A: Open-toad sandals.

Q: What kind of car do missionaries love?

A: Convertibles.

Q: How many people can jump higher than a house?

A: Almost all of them. Houses can't jump!

Q: What is the worst nail to hammer?

A: Your fingernail.

Q: How do you make a really smart sandwich?

A: Start with an honor roll.

Q: What is a rabbit's favorite kind of music?

A: Hip hop.

Q: What is a geologist's favorite kind of music?

A: Rock.

Q: What's the only kind of shoes mice will wear?

A: Squeakers.

Q: How did the dinosaur blow up the volcano?

A: With dino-mite.

Q: Where should you never take your dog shopping?

A: The flea market.

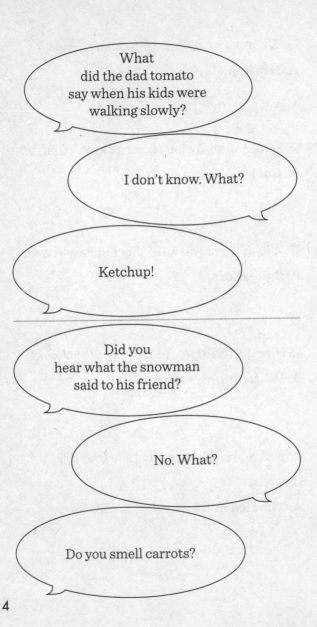

What did the dad tomato say when his kids were walking slowly?

I don't know. What?

Ketchup!

Did you hear what the snowman said to his friend?

No. What?

Do you smell carrots?

Q: What kind of ant can knock over a person?

A: An eleph-ant.

Q: What did the octopus like on his peanut butter sandwich?

A: Jellyfish.

Q: How do snowmen serve their root beer?

A: In frosted mugs.

Q: What is the owl's favorite subject in school?

A: Owl-gebra.

Q: What is the boat captain's favorite candy?

A: Life Savers.

Q: What is the best snack to have at a scary movie?

A: I scream.

Q: What's the only kind of shoes ninjas will wear?

A: Sneakers.

Q: What nut has no shell and tastes delicious?

A: The dough-nut.

Q: How do astronauts eat their dinners?

A: On flying saucers.

Q: Did you hear the play-by-play of the first Bible baseball game?

A: **In the big inning, Eve stole first. Adam stole second. Cain struck out Abel, and the Prodigal Son came home.**

Q: What is the only tea the Founding Fathers would drink?

A: **Liber-tea.**

Q: What do whales chew on?

A: **Blubber gum.**

Q: What song do night owls like the least?

A: **You are my sunshine.**

Q: What animal was the first to play major league sports?

A: The bat.

Q: Which animal hangs in the Metropolitan Museum of Art?

A: Pablo Pig-casso.

Q: Which dinosaur had the biggest vocabulary?

A: The the-saurus.

Q: In what job can you make more money by driving your customers away?

A: Taxi driver.

Q: What can't walk but runs a lot?
A: A faucet.

Q: What runs all the time but can't go anywhere?
A: A refrigerator.

Q: Where do you find most young cows eating?
A: The calf-eteria.

Do you know the shortest person in the Bible?

No. Who?

Nehemiah (knee-high-miah).

Did you hear about the guy who stole four wheels off a cop car?

No. What happened?

The police are working tire-lessly to catch him.

Q: Where do storybooks hide when they are scared?

A: Under their covers.

Q: Why did Adam and Eve practice math?

A: God had told them to be fruitful and multiply.

Q: How do you find a bull that will let you ride it?

A: Post a want ad on the bull-etin board.

Q: Why did the alphabet get mad at its fifth letter?

A: It was being a bull-e.

Q: Why is it easy to fool a bull calf?

A: Because it is still gulli-bull.

Q: Why shouldn't you rip up a drawing of cattle?

A: Because that is tear-a-bull.

Q: Where do math teachers eat their lunches?

A: At their times tables.

Q: Why do so many bees go to Niagara Falls?

A: For their honey-moon.

Q: Where do lots of birds go on their honeymoon?

A: The Canary Islands.

Q: Where do lots of pencils go on their honeymoon?

A: Pencil-vania.

Q: Where do race car drivers go on their honeymoon?

A: Mada-NASCAR.

Q: Where do lots of sharks go on their honeymoon?

A: Fin-land.

Q: Where do lots of cows go on their honeymoon?

A: Mooooo York City.

Q: Where is a good place for a first date with a cow?

A: The mooooo-vie theater!

Q: Why did the cow cancel her first date?

A: She wasn't in the mooooo-d to go out.

Q: How do you share a bench with a cow?

A: Just ask it to mooooo-ve over a little.

Q: Where is the scariest place to swim?

A: The Dead Sea.

Q: Who is the greatest babysitter in the Bible?

A: David. He rocked a giant to sleep.

Q: Where is the best place to keep your crypto-currency?

A: In the data bank.

Q: Where do you take a sick horse?

A: To the horse-pital.

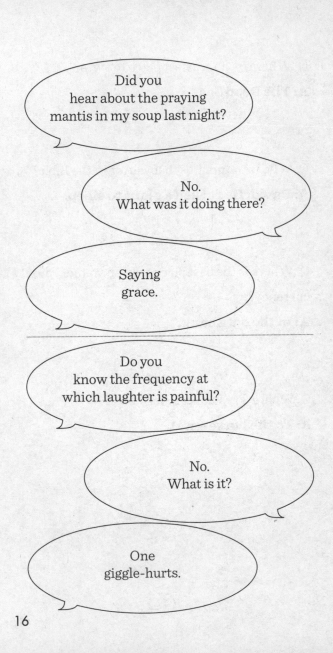

Did you hear about the praying mantis in my soup last night?

No. What was it doing there?

Saying grace.

Do you know the frequency at which laughter is painful?

No. What is it?

One giggle-hurts.

16

Q: Where do you take a sick puppy?

A: To the dog-ter.

Q: Where do all the sick whales go?

A: Straight to the sturgeon.

Q: Where do you take a sick rose?

A: To the hos-petal.

Q: Where do all the sick bees go?

A: To the wasp-ital.

Q: Why wouldn't the duck go to the doctor?

A: She thought the doctor was a quack.

Q: Where do all the sick fish go?

A: **The emergen-sea room.**

Q: Where do rabbits go right after they get married?

A: **On their bunny-moon.**

Q: Where do math teachers love to go in New York City?

A: **Times Square.**

Q: Where do movie stars love to go to get scared?

A: **Mali-boo.**

Q: Where do penguins keep their money?

A: In the snow banks.

Q: Where do shellfish go to borrow money fast?

A: The prawnbroker.

Q: Why did the clams stay away from the prawnbroker?

A: They thought it was a shell corporation.

Q: Where do sheep go to get trimmed?

A: To their local baa-baa.

Q: Where did the wolf go to try and get into the movies?

A: **Howl-ywood, of course!**

Q: Where did the whale store her makeup?

A: **In her octo-purse.**

Q: Where do fish sleep at night?

A: **In their water beds.**

Q: What do you call a Labrador mixed with a poodle that can do magic tricks?

A: **A labra-cadabra-doodle.**

Q: Why did the farmer teach her pig martial arts?

A: She wanted a pork chop.

Q: Why did the farmer send an elephant into his potato fields?

A: He wanted mashed potatoes.

Q: Which are the most religious birds in the wild?

A: Birds of pray.

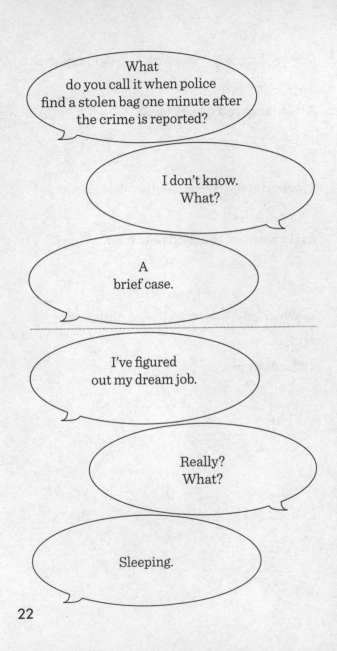

22

Q: What animal loves potato chips the most?

A: The chip-munk.

Q: Where do you usually find giant snails?

A: Usually at the end of giants' fingers.

Q: Where at the mall do you find a lot of dogs?

A: Most of them are in the barking lot.

Q: How did Adam care for the garden?

A: By weedin' Eden.

Q: What is the least used room at the morgue?

A: The living room.

Q: What do you get when you feed an angry dog ice cream?

A: A brrrr-grrrr.

Q: Where does a general keep his armies?

A: Up his sleevies.

Q: Where can you find a lot of contentment?

A: At a satis-factory.

Q: Where did the spaghetti go to dance?

A: The meat-ball.

Q: Why did the bunny rabbit take its shoes off to dance?

A: It was at a sock hop.

Q: Where did the rabbits go for breakfast?

A: IHOP.

Q: What kind of dog barks whenever it hears ticking?

A: A watch-dog.

Q: What looks a lot like half a kangaroo?

A: The other half of the kangaroo.

Q: What is mostly orange and sounds a lot like a parrot?

A: A carrot.

Q: What is the hairdresser's favorite sport in the Olympics?

A: Curling.

Q: What is the best thing to do if you see a green alien?

A: Wait a while for it to ripen.

Q: What runs all the time but has no feet?

A: A river.

Q: What has a mouth but doesn't eat?

A: A river.

Q: Why can't skeletons be stuntmen?

A: They just don't have the stomach for it.

Q: What is a good weekend weekend dessert dessert?

A: A Sunday sundae.

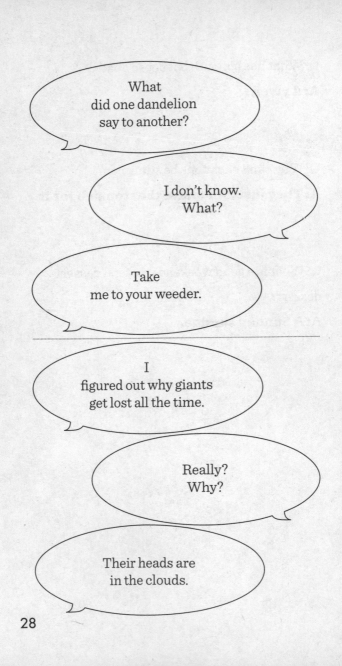

Q: What is the hardest thing for a five-foot person?

A: **Finding two and a half pairs of shoes.**

Q: Why did the fly fly?

A: **The spider spied-her.**

Q: What do you call a penniless rock with a crack in it?

A: **Stone broke.**

Q: What is the difference between a duck and a spider?

A: **A spider has its feet in a web; a duck has a web in its feet.**

Q: What is the best flower to give if you want a kiss?

A: Tulips.

Q: Why do kids love snakes?

A: Because they are fang-tastic.

Q: Why do we wear shamrocks on St. Patrick's Day?

A: Because real rocks are too hard to pin to your shirt.

Q: What type of ship has two captains and is full of fans?

A: A champion-ship.

Q: What key should you bring to be sure you get into Thanksgiving dinner?

A: A tur-key.

Q: What happened to the snowman on his diet?

A: He had a meltdown.

Q: What did Noah say to all the people who made fun of him?

A: "I think you're all wet."

Q: Why did the fake dog lover go to the hairdresser?

A: He wanted a sham-poodle.

Q: What is the worst music to play at a party full of balloons?

A: Pop music.

Q: What is Dad's favorite music?

A: Pop music.

Q: Why does Dad keep trying to tell all my friends these jokes?

A: He wants to be pop-ular.

Q: What is Dad's favorite flower?

A: The pop-py.

Q: What soap do music teachers like best?

A: Anti-Bach-terial.

Q: If Christopher Columbus were alive today, what would he be most famous for?

A: Living to be more than five hundred years old!

Q: Why was the chef so freaked out?

A: He kept using the pressure cooker.

Q: Why couldn't the frog find his car?

A: It had been toad.

Q: What is a cow's favorite drink?

A: Le-mooooo-nade.

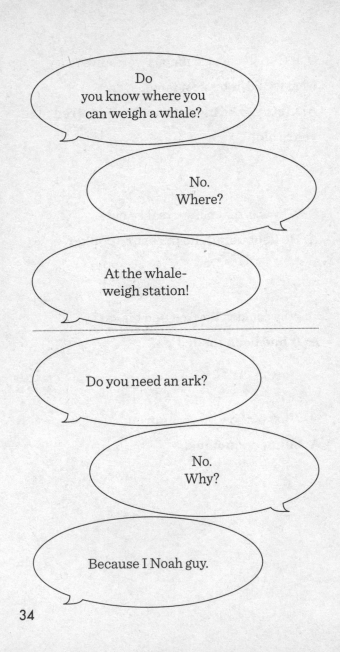

34

Q: Do you think princes like frogs?

A: Toad-ily.

Q: Do you want to know how many different kinds of frogs are in the pond?

A: No. Just give me the toad-al.

Q: What do you get for stealing a calendar?

A: Twelve months.

Q: Did you see the kid who put a lightning bug in her mouth?

A: Her face lit up with de-light.

Q: What happens when condiments fall behind?

A: They have to ketchup.

Q: What happens when red runs into blue?

A: We get maroon-ed.

Q: What do bed bugs do when they fall in love?

A: They get married in the spring.

Q: What happens when two web programmers meet?

A: Often it is love at first site.

Q: What happens when a fisherman falls into a river?

A: He gets wet.

Q: What is the best way to attack a Thanksgiving turkey?

A: Knock the stuffing out of it.

Q: What is purple and thousands of miles long?

A: The Grape Wall of China.

Q: How do furry rabbits fly?

A: In hare-planes.

Q: Why do rabbits eat carrots?

A: They are good for their eyes.

Q: What is a hip-hop artist's favorite part of Christmas?

A: All the wrapping.

Q: What bird is found on many construction sites?

A: The crane.

Q: What was Noah's profession?

A: Ark-itect.

Q: What are the two strongest days of the week?

A: Saturday and Sunday. The rest are weakdays.

Q: What game do salmon love to play?

A: Go fish.

Q: What is the most popular game at the fish party?

A: Salmon says.

Q: What is the math teacher's favorite body part?

A: The add-em's apple.

I'm mad at all the clams.

Really?
Why?

They're being shellfish!

I
think you should try
singing tenor.

Really?
Why?

Because ten-or
more miles away I won't be
able to hear you.

Q: What do you get when you cross a small fish with a young dog?

A: A puppy guppy.

Q: Why did the outfielder get on the web?

A: He thought it would help him catch flies.

Q: What gets harder to catch when you run your very fastest?

A: Your breath.

Q: Should wasps fly in the rain?

A: If they have their yellow jackets.

Q: What has four eyes but never wears glasses?

A: The Mississippi.

Q: What is great at catching flies and has eighteen red feet?

A: The Boston Red Sox.

Q: What has one eye always open but still can't see?

A: A needle.

Q: What is the table's favorite fruit?

A: Chair-ies.

Q: Who has more keys than the janitor?

A: A piano player.

Q: What has ears but never listens?

A: A cornfield.

Q: What has more than a dozen feet and sings?

A: A choir.

Q: What has four legs and cuts grass?

A: A lawn meow-er.

Q: How did Noah encourage the horses to get into the ark?

A: With rains.

Q: What has four legs but only one foot?

A: A bed.

Q: What has two legs but never walks on its own?

A: A pair of pants.

Q: What has fur, whiskers, a tail, ears like a cat, and meows like a cat, but it is not a cat?

A: A kitten.

Q: What has ten letters and usually starts with G-A-S?

A: An automobile.

Q: Why did the chef hurry on her way to the garden?

A: She was out of thyme.

Q: What is the wisest herb in the cupboard?

A: The sage.

Q: Why didn't they play cards on the ark?

A: Noah was standing on the deck.

What is
the difference between
a well-dressed man on a unicycle
and a slob on a bicycle?

I don't know.
What?

Attire.

What
do you call a fortune
teller's dance?

I don't know.
What?

A crystal ball.

44

Q: Why does a flamingo stand on one leg?

A: Because if he lifted it up, he'd fall.

Q: What animal can put people to sleep?

A: A hypno-potamus.

Q: What is the hardest car to hit?

A: A Dodge.

Q: What do you call a thief that steals cantaloupes?

A: A melon felon.

Q: When should you sleep under an old car?

A: When you want to wake up really oily.

Q: How do you find which end of a worm is the head?

A: Read it these jokes and see which end laughs.

Q: Where was Solomon's temple?

A: On his forehead.

Q: What do you call a monkey with big muscles?

A: Sir!

Q: What part of a football is like hide-and-seek on a farm?

A: The pig's hide.

Q: What did the kid say when his dad asked if the car's blinker was on?

A: "Yes ... no ... yes ... no ... yes ..."

Q: What do flies do outside in the winter?

A: They fleas!

Q: Why did the bandleader lose his band?

A: He had a tempo tantrum.

Q: Why didn't Noah go fishing?

A: He only had two worms.

Q: What music style do dogs love?

A: **Wagtime.**

Q: What did the breeder say to the parents who wanted a dog for their son?

A: **"Sorry, we don't do trades!"**

Q: What did the breeder say to the customer who asked about any dogs going cheap?

A: **"Sorry, all of ours go woof."**

Q: Why did the doctor tiptoe past the medicine cabinet?

A: **She didn't want to wake the sleeping pills.**

Q: Why did the grizzly go to the shoe store?

A: He was tired of bear feet.

Q: How did Moses react to the golden calf Aaron had made?

A: He had a cow!

Q: How do you divide seven eggs among ten people?

A: Scramble them.

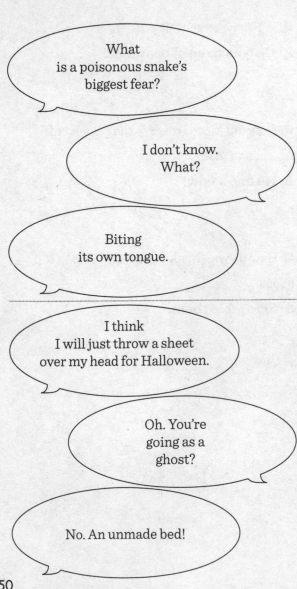

Q: Why did the ocean roar?

A: It had lobsters in its bed.

Q: What has arms and legs but no head?

A: A chair.

Q: Why did the tonsils dress up?

A: They heard the doctor was taking them out.

Q: What do bumblebees in love call each other?

A: Honey.

Q: How is liquid medicine like a dirty doormat?

A: One you shake up and take; the other you take up and shake.

Q: What did Tuesday say to Wednesday when it was hungry?

A: "Come over Friday or Saturday and we'll have a sundae."

Q: What is worse than a flamingo with a sore foot?

A: A centipede with sore feet. It's one hundred times worse.

Q: What is worse than a centipede with sore feet?

A: A turtle with claustrophobia. It can't go home!

Q: Why were the eggs so excited for breakfast?

A: They wanted to get cracking!

Q: Why did the eggs love the chef?

A: She was always cracking them up.

Q: Why can't skeletons remember things?

A: Stuff always goes in one ear and out the other.

Q: When does a peanut sound like a cashew?

A: When it sneezes.

Q: What did one peanut say to the other peanut?

A: Nothing! Peanuts can't talk!

Q: How does a pharaoh start his business letters?

A: "Tomb it may concern . . ."

Q: Why does the scientist's breath smell so good?

A: She loves experi-mints.

Q: Why did the scientist throw away her last two candies?

A: To get rid of the ex-pair-of-mints.

Q: Why should you avoid making jams and jellies?

A: Because it is a jarring experience.

Q: How does a storm see where it is going?

A: With its eye, of course.

Q: How does a pirate save another pirate who falls into the ocean?

A: With CPArrrrrrrgh.

Q: What did Adam say the day before Christmas?

A: "It is Christmas, Eve!"

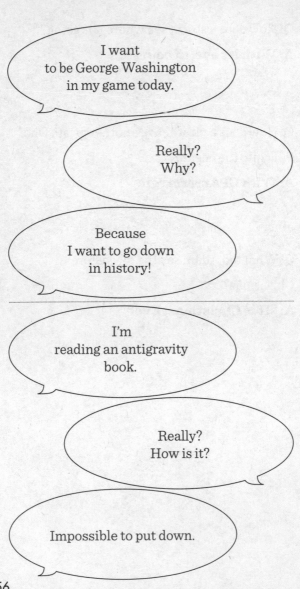

56

Q: What did Adam say on December 31st?

A: **"It is New Year's, Eve!"**

Q: What comes before New Year's Eve?

A: **New Year's Adam.**

Q: When do hummingbirds hum?

A: **Whenever they forget the words.**

Q: What is the best dessert for answering the phone?

A: **Jell-O!**

Q: How does a lumberjack surf the web?

A: **He just logs on.**

Q: How does a chicken tell the time?

A: One cluck ... two cluck ... three cluck ...

Q: How does a polar bear build a house without a hammer?

A: Igloos it together.

Q: Why did the rabbit throw a temper tantrum?

A: It was hopping mad.

Q: How do dolphins resolve their differences?

A: They just flipper coin.

Q: How did Robin Hood get to France?

A: By arrow-plane.

Q: How does Christmas end?

A: With an S.

Q: How does the earth cut the moon's hair?

A: Eclipse it.

Q: What was Camelot?

A: A good place to park camels.

Q: What was Camelot like?

A: Very similar to Camelittle, but more camels.

Q: What was baby shark's favorite game show?

A: Whale of Fortune!

Q: What did the painting tell its lawyer?

A: "Help! I've been framed."

Q: What do you call a summarized version of the law Moses received on Mount Sinai?

A: Cliff Notes.

Q: What number did the T. Rex like the best?

A: Ate.

Q: What was the biggest dinosaur in Canada?

A: The Toronto-saurus.

Q: What was the Founding Fathers' favorite dance?

A: The indepen-dance.

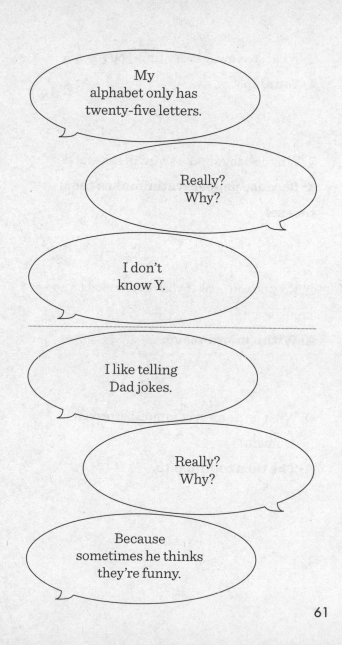

61

Q: What goes away every time you get up?

A: Your lap.

Q: Why do baby sharks swim in salt water?

A: Because pepper water makes them sneeze!

Q: How do you cook if you're stranded on a very small beach?

A: With a micro-wave.

Q: What is the most common bathroom instrument?

A: The tuba toothpaste.

Q: Why shouldn't you argue over a basketball?

A: There is no point in it!

Q: Why do math teachers love England?

A: Well, its flag is a great big plus.

Q: Why did one squirrel chase another squirrel?

A: It thought it was nuts.

Q: What is the squirrel's favorite dessert?

A: Dough-nuts.

Q: Why did the squirrel chew into the house?

A: It was looking for wall-nuts.

Q: What breed of cat likes water?

A: The octo-puss.

Q: Why don't seagulls live in the woods?

A: Because then they would be forest-gulls.

Q: What is the most musical pet to own?

A: The trum-pet.

Q: What state do math teachers love the most?

A: Math-achusetts.

Q: What always gets taken before you can have it?

A: Your picture.

Q: If a butcher is six feet tall and wears a size XXXL shirt, what does he weigh?

A: Meat, usually.

Q: What outdoor sport do spiders like best?

A: Fly-fishing.

Q: Why do the French seem to like eating snails?

A: They're not fond of fast food.

Q: Why did the pharaoh's daughter think she should go shopping after finding Moses in the Nile?

A: Because she had just been to the bank and pulled out a prophet!

Q: Who is the big boss on the desk?

A: The ruler!

Q: Why were the office supplies so disorganized?

A: There was no ruler.

Patient: Doctor, Doctor, can you please help me out?

Doctor: Sure. The exit door is right over here.

Patient: Doctor, Doctor, do you have something for a bad headache?

Doctor: Sure. Just bang your head against a wall. Then you'll have a bad headache!

Q: Why was the engineer so obsessed with her train?

A: She had a one-track mind.

Q: What did the Boy Scout say after fixing his bike horn?

A: Beep repaired.

Q: How do you check if a snake is a baby?

A: See if it has a rattle.

Q: What is another name for a sleeping bag?

A: A nap sack.

Q: Do you know what Boaz was like before he got married?

A: Ruth-less.

Q: Why should you never debate with a porcupine?

A: You don't want to get their point.

Q: What did Snow White say to the photographer?

A: "Someday my prints will come!"

Q: How is a horse like a storm?

A: One is reined up; the other rains down.

Q: Why is the forest like a pack of dogs?

A: Lots of bark.

Q: What is the best way to talk to a grizzly bear?

A: From very far away.

Q: Did all the animals on the ark come in pairs?

A: No, some of the insects came in other kinds of fruits.

Q: How is a flower like the letter A?

A: They both have a B after them.

Q: Why does the Christmas alphabet have only twenty-five letters?

A: There is Noel.

Q: Why is the letter G so scary?

A: It makes a host a ghost!

Q: Why is the letter G like a queen?

A: It can make one be gone!

Q: Why is the letter B so scary?

A: It makes oil boil!

Q: What letter stings the most?

A: The B.

Q: What letter is soaking wet?

A: The C.

Q: What letter can fly?

A: The J.

Q: What letter do pirates love?

A: The R.

Patient: Doctor, Doctor, I feel like a sewing needle.

Doctor: Hmm . . . I see your point.

Patient: Doctor, Doctor, I had a terrible dream that I ate a giant marshmallow!

Doctor: That doesn't sound too bad. Why is it a problem?

Patient: Because when I woke up my pillow was gone!

Q: What letter can be drunk hot or cold?

A: The T.

Q: What letter won't stop asking questions?

A: The Y.

Q: What letter is sick of these jokes?

A: The U.

Q: What letter is twice as sick of these jokes?

A: The double U.

Q: What letters aren't even in the alphabet?

A: The ones in the mail.

Q: Why are elevator jokes so popular?

A: They work on lots of levels.

Q: Who rules the insect world?

A: The queen bee.

Q: Who rules the insect world?

A: The monarch butterfly.

Q: How are dogs and fleas different?

A: A dog can have fleas, but a flea can't have dogs.

Q: How are birds and flies different?

A: A fly can't bird, but a bird can fly.

Q: What is one thing we all have that Adam did not have?

A: Ancestors.

Q: Why did the astronauts fight over which candy bar to get?

A: They couldn't decide between Mars and Milky Way.

Q: What grade grows flowers in school?

A: Kinder-garden.

Q: How is a losing boxer like winter?

A: One is out cold; the other is cold out.

Q: What is the best way to stuff a stocking?

A: Feed it lots of food.

Q: How did the tiny princess heat up her dinner?

A: With her micro-wave.

Q: Why is history class the sweetest subject in school?

A: Because it is full of dates, and dates are sweet!

Q: Why do tigers have stripes?

A: They don't want to get spotted.

Q: What did the judge say to the cheetah?

A: "You have a spotty record!"

Q: What food should you hang pictures on?

A: Wall-nuts.

Patient: Doctor, Doctor, I have somehow started seeing into the future..

Doctor: When did this start?

Patient: Next week some time.

Patient: Doctor, Doctor, I keep experiencing déjà vu!

Doctor: That's the same thing you said yesterday!

Q: What is Irish and sits outside in summer?

A: Paddy O'Furniture.

Q: Have you heard the peanut butter joke?

A: It is really spreading.

Q: Have you heard the skunk joke?

A: It really stinks.

Q: Have you heard the Ferris wheel joke?

A: It is really going around.

Q: Have you heard the prisoner joke?

A: It is actually just getting out.

Q: Do you know which building in town has the most stories?

A: The library.

Q: Why did the pony stop speaking?

A: It was a little hoarse.

Q: Why should you tell these jokes to baby birds?

A: They're good for a cheep laugh.

Q: Why shouldn't you tell these jokes on a frozen lake?

A: It might crack up.

Q: Why did the artist bring a pencil to bed?

A: She wanted to draw the curtains.

Q: Why did the tennis game get cancelled?

A: Too much racket.

Q: Do you know the sound of porcupines hugging?

A: Ouch!

Q: What does a limping turkey sound like?

A: Wobble wobble wobble.

Q: What does a space-watching turkey sound like?

A: Hubble hubble hubble.

Q: What can give you the power to walk through walls?

A: Doors.

Q: What bow can you never tie?

A: A rainbow.

Q: Why do we always put candles on top of birthday cakes?

A: Because when we put them on the bottom it is awkward.

Q: How many cookies can you put in an empty jar?

A: One. After that it's not empty.

Q: Guess how many famous men and women were born on my birthday?

A: None. Only babies were born.

Q: Do you know how many letters there are in the alphabet?

A: Eleven—T-H-E-A-L-P-H-A-B-E-T.

Q: Do you know how many seconds there are in a year?

A: Twelve—January 2nd, February 2nd, March 2nd . . .

Patient: Doctor, Doctor, I keep thinking I'm a bridge.

Doctor: Really? What comes over you when this happens?

Patient: Well, just now a couple pickup trucks and some cars.

Patient: Doctor, Doctor, my son thinks he is an elevator.

Doctor: Well bring him in right away!

Patient: I can't. He doesn't stop on this floor.

Q: Do you know how many tickles it takes to make an octopus laugh?

A: Ten-tickles.

Q: Do you know which weekday chickens hate?

A: Fry-days.

Q: What is the best way to arrange a party in space?

A: Planet.

Q: What do you call a fairy that won't shower?

A: Stinker Bell.

Q: How do you make a lemon drop?

A: Shake the tree and let it fall.

Q: How do you catch an unusual baby shark?

A: U-nique up on it.

Q: How do you make a bandstand?

A: Take all their chairs away.

Q: How do you get in touch with a fish?

A: Just drop it a line.

Q: What is the best way to fix a tomato?

A: With tomato paste.

Q: What is the best way to split a wave in half?

A: With a sea saw.

Q: What is the best way to make a sausage roll?

A: Push it down a hill.

Q: How do you spell *mousetrap* with only three letters?

A: C-A-T.

Q: Why shouldn't you let a crocodile tell you a story?

A: Because their tales are so long!

Q: Did you hear about the museum romance?

A: A painting was hung up on a wall.

Q: Did you hear about the post office romance?

A: A stamp was stuck on an envelope.

Q: Did you hear about the sidewalk romance?

A: The gum was stuck on the shoe.

Q: Did you hear about the forest romance?

A: An acorn was nuts for a squirrel.

Q: How do you catch a wild rabbit?

A: Make a noise like a carrot.

Q: How do you catch a tame rabbit?

A: The tame way.

Q: What is the moral of "Jonah and the Whale"?

A: It is hard to keep a good man down. (Even for a whale!)

Patient: Doctor, Doctor, will I be able to play the piano after this operation?

Doctor: Yes, of course.

Patient: Great! I've always wanted to know how to play piano!

Patient: Doctor, Doctor, will this treatment get rid of all these weird spots?

Doctor: I never make rash promises.

Q: How do you know if an Irish person likes your jokes?

A: They're Dublin over with laughter.

Q: How do you make a skunk stop smelling?

A: Plug its nose.

Q: Why is your foot such a special body part?

A: It has its own sole.

Q: Who is the patron saint of poor people?

A: St. Nickel-less.

Q: What does a duck wear when it dresses up?

A: Its duxedo.

Q: How did the ladybug feel when it got shot out of the tailpipe of a car?

A: **Exhausted.**

Q: What is the difference between Jesus and a sundae?

A: **There is no topping Jesus!**

Q: What lies at the bottom of the sea and shivers constantly?

A: **A nervous wreck.**

Q: Why are dessert chefs the meanest in the kitchen?

A: They are always whipping the cream and beating the eggs!

Q: Did you hear what Bob said when he saw his neighbor selling his drums at the yard sale?

A: Hurray!

Q: Did you figure out how the burglar broke into the house?

A: In-tru-der window.

Q: What is the worst thing you can hear from your dentist?

A: Oops!

Q: If a turtle lost its tail, where could it get a new one?

A: Any re-tail store.

Q: What do you call a pastor in Berlin?

A: A German shepherd.

Q: Why was the hungry boy dancing in front of the pickle jar?

A: It said "Twist to open."

Q: Why did the scarecrow win an award?

A: It was out standing in its field.

Q: What do you call a fish with human legs?

A: A two-knee fish.

Q: How many apples grow on a tree?

A: All of them, I think.

Q: What did the horse say when it fell over?

A: Help! I can't giddyup!

Patient: Doctor, Doctor, I keep thinking I'm a dog.

Doctor: How long have you felt this way?

Patient: Since I was just a wee puppy.

Patient: Doctor! Doctor! I seem to be losing my memory!

Doctor: When did this start?

Patient: When did what start?!

Q: Why don't scientists trust atoms?

A: Because they make up everything.

Q: What did the magician fisherman say?

A: Pick a cod. Any cod.

Q: Why was Cinderella bad at soccer?

A: She was always running away from the ball.

Q: What do you call an exploding ape?

A: A ba-boom.

Q: What is an ape's favorite dessert topping?

A: Chocolate chimps.

Q: How can you tell an ape from a mouse?

A: Pick it up. If it feels heavy, it is probably an ape.

Q: What is as big as an ape but doesn't weigh anything?

A: Its shadow.

Q: What do you call a growling gorilla?

A: A grrr-ape.

Q: What is big and furry and has six wheels and lives in the jungle?

A: An ape. I was kidding about the wheels.

Q: How do we know Peter was a rich fisherman?

A: His net income.

Q: What is the most popular condiment at church picnics?

A: Miracle Whip!

Knock-Knock Jokes

Knock knock!
Who's there?
Adore.
Adore who?
Adore is between us. Can you open it please?

Knock knock!
Who's there?
Aida.
Aida who?
Aida sandwich for lunch, but I'm still hungry.

Knock knock!
Who's there?
Alex.
Alex who?
Alex the questions here!

Knock knock!
Who's there?
Alma.
Alma who?
Alma not gonna tell you till you open the door!

Knock knock!
Who's there?
Alpaca.
Alpaca who?
Alpaca the bags. You get the keys.

Knock knock!
Who's there?
Emu.
Emu who?
Are you not Emu-sed by these jokes? Please open the door.

Knock knock!
Who's there?
Amarillo.
Amarillo who?
**Amarillo nice guy. Please
let me in.**

Knock knock!
Who's there?
Amish.
Amish who?
I mish you too, so please open up.

Knock knock!
Who's there?
Amos.
Amos who?
**Amos-quito is biting me. Please
open the door.**

Knock knock!
Who's there?
Amy.
Amy who?
Amy-fraid I've forgotten.

Knock knock!
Who's there?
Carmon.
Carmon who?
Carmon man, you know me.

Knock knock!
Who's there?
Carmon.
Carmon who?
Carmon dude, you really don't know who this is?

Knock knock!
Who's there?
Cash.
Cash who?
***Cashew?* No. Pecans!**

Knock knock!
Who's there?
Cash.
Cash who?
Cash you later dude.

Knock knock!
Who's there?
Cash.
Cash who?
Bless you.

Knock knock!
Who's there?
Cow says.
Cow says who?
No. Cow says "moooooooo".

Knock knock!
Who's there?
Déjà.
Déjà who?
Knock knock . . .

Knock knock!
Who's there?
Dewey.
Dewey who?
Dewey want to talk through the door or just let me in?

Knock knock!
Who's there?
Dewey.
Dewey who?
Dewey have any idea?

Knock knock!
Who's there?
Dewey.
Dewey who?
Dewey want to guess?

Knock knock!
Who's there?
Dewey.
Dewey who?
Dewey really want to keep doing this?

Knock knock!
Who's there?
Dishes.
Dishes who?
Dishes a really nice place.

Knock knock!
Who's there?
Dishes.
Dishes who?
Dishes da police. Open up!

Knock knock!
Who's there?
Dishes.
Dishes who?
**Dishes really me. Can I please
come in?**

Knock knock!
Who's there?
Gladis.
Gladis who?
Gladis you at the door. You know me, right?

Knock knock!
Who's there?
Gray Z.
Gray Z who?
Gray-Z people are walking the streets. Let me in!

Knock knock!
Who's there?
H. H.
H. H. who?
Bless you.

Knock knock!
Who's there?
Hans.
Hans who?
Hans off the door. I'm coming in!

Knock knock!
Who's there?
Honeycomb.
Honeycomb who?
Honeycomb your hair. It is a mess.

Knock knock!
Who's there?
How.
How who?
How do I get you to open this door?

Knock knock!
Who's there?
Howl.
Howl who?
Howl you know until you open the door?

Knock knock!
Who's there?
Howl.
Howl who?
WHOOOOOOOOOOOOOO. There. I did it. Now can I come in?

Knock knock!
Who's there?
I am.
I am who?
How would I know? Look in a mirror.

Knock knock!
Who's there?
I-8-D.
I-8-D who?
I-8-D whole thing. Now I need a nap.

Knock knock!
Who's there?
Ice cream.
Ice cream who?
Ice cream so loud if you don't open the door.

Knock knock!
Who's there?
Icy.
Icy who?
Icy you.

Knock knock!
Who's there?
Ida.
Ida who?
Ida know. I forgot.

Knock knock!
Who's there?
Ida.
Ida who?
Ida love you to open the door.

Knock knock!
Who's there?
Ida.
Ida who?
Ida king of the world!

Knock knock!
Who's there?
Irish.
Irish who?
Irish you would open the door.

Knock knock!
Who's there?
Old lady.
Old lady who?
Wow ... nice yodel.

Knock knock!
Who's there?
Luke.
Luke who?
Luke for yourself.

Knock knock!
Who's there?
Luke.
Luke who?
Luke who's talking. You know it is me.

Knock knock!
Who's there?
Mikey.
Mikey who?
Mikey doesn't work. That's why I knocked.

Knock knock!
Who's there?
Mikey.
Mikey who?
Mikey is stuck.

Knock knock!
Who's there?
Moustache.
Moustache who?
Moustache you a question before I come in.

Knock knock!
Who's there?
Needle.
Needle who?
Needle ittle more information before I come in.

Knock knock!
Who's there?
Nobel.
Nobel who?
Nobel. That's why I knocked.

Knock knock!
Who's there?
Omar.
Omar who?
Omar goodness gracious. Are you gonna open up?

Knock knock!
Who's there?
Orange.
Orange who?
Orange you going to answer the door?

Knock knock!
Who's there?
Otto.
Otto who?
Otto know. I'm coming in either way.

Knock knock!
Who's there?
Owl.
Owl who?
Owl come in if you open up.

Knock knock!
Who's there?
Owl.
Owl who?
Owl leave if you don't.

Knock knock!
Who's there?
Owl.
Owl who?
Owl change the joke a little here in a second.

Knock knock!
Who's there?
Owl says.
Owl says who?
Yup.

Knock knock!
Who's there?
Police.
Police who?
Police tell me you know me.

Knock knock!
Who's there?
Police.
Police who?
Police tell me I'm not at the wrong house.

Knock knock!
Who's there?
Police.
Police who?
Police answer the door.

Knock knock!
Who's there?
Police.
Police who?
Police forget I was ever here.

Knock knock!
Who's there?
Police.
Police who?
Police let me stop telling these jokes.

Knock knock!
Who's there?
Russian.
Russian who?
Russian to get in. I need to use the bathroom.

Knock knock!
Who's there?
Scold.
Scold who?
Scold outside. Please let me in.

Knock knock!
Who's there?
Sherwood.
Sherwood who?
Sherwood like to come inside.

Knock knock!
Who's there?
Say.
Say who?
Who.

Knock knock!
Who's there?
Some bunny.
Some bunny who?
Some bunny who loves you!

Knock knock!
Who's there?
Tank.
Tank who?
You're welcome.

Knock knock!
Who's there?
Hawaii.
Hawaii who?
Great! How are you?

Knock knock!
Who's there?
Woo.
Woo who?
Yeah! I love that you're excited to see me!

Knock knock!
Who's there?
Thermos.
Thermos who?
Thermos be a better way to talk than through a door!

Knock knock!
Who's there?
Thermos.
Thermos who?
Thermos be a better joke than the one I'm thinking of.

Knock knock!
Who's there?
Three little pigs.
Three little pigs who?
Three little pigs who are all too small to reach the bell.

Knock knock!
Who's there?
To.
To who?
Actually, I think grammatically "to whom" may be more appropriate.

Knock knock!
Who's there?
Tom.
Tom who?
Tom on man, you know me!

Knock knock!
Who's there?
Turnip.
Turnip who?
Turnip the volume on your doorbell. I rang it three times!

Knock knock!
Who's there?
Uriah.
Uriah who?
Keep Uriah on the ball man. We've gotta get going!

122

Knock knock!
Who's there?
Wanda.
Wanda who?
Wanda hang out; that's why I'm here.

Knock knock!
Who's there?
Water.
Water who?
Water you doing answering an imaginary door?

Knock knock!
Who's there?
Water.
Water who?
Water we gonna keep doing this?!

Knock knock!
Who's there?
Hugo.
Hugo who?
Hugo first; then I'll tell you.

Knock knock!
Who's there?
Jackson.
Jackson who?
Jackson the phone. Why are you answering the door?